The FAMILY CHRISTMAS BUCKET JOURNAL

100+ Activities to Celebrate the Most Wonderful Time of the Year

©2021 by My Bucket Journals LLC
Designed and printed in the USA. All rights reserved.

ISBN: 978-1-63933-054-6
Printer: My Bucket Journals, LLC
PO Box 310, Hutto, Texas 78634

This publication may not be reproduced stored or transmitted in whole or in part, in any form or by any means, electronic, mechanical or otherwise, without prior written consent from the publisher and author.

Brief quotations may be included in a review. If in PDF form, it may be stored on your computer and you may keep one online digital copy. This publication may be printed for personal use only.

Disclaimer
The information in this book is based on the author's opinion, knowledge and experience. The publisher and the author will not be held liable for the use or misuse of the information contained herein.

Disclosure
This book may contain affiliate links. If you click through an affiliate link to a third-party website and make a purchase, the author may receive a small commission.

Cover photo ©DepositPhotos

This book belongs to

_____
If found please call

_____

How to Use The Family Christmas Bucket Journal

Make new family traditions and celebrate the season. The Family Christmas Bucket Journal will help you find, plan, and journal about your holiday experiences together. Make each activity count and record the memories.

There is room to plan and journal 40 Christmas activities in this bucket journal.

These are grouped into six different topics. Decide as a family whether you're focusing on one category each week or interspersing the range of ideas throughout the season.

- Crafty Ideas
- Ways to Give
- Activities in the Kitchen
- Activities in the Community
- Making Family Traditions
- The Reason for the Season

When you've decided on the activities you want to do, go to an open page and begin planning the day or evening. There is space for adding information about reservations, budget, and your notes to make this a memorable family time together.

After the activity, take time to journal about the experience. What was fun, how did you feel, what activity will become a family tradition?

After the season, you'll have a collection of memories to look back on again and again.

Table of Contents

Crafty Ideas – start on page 4
We've got you covered with nineteen crafty ideas for making wreaths, ornaments, handmade gifts decorations, cards, and more.

Ways to Give – start on page 7
Give back this season when you choose some of the eighteen ideas to help others. Ideas include sending a care package, working at a food back, or visiting someone who is lonely.

Activities In the Kitchen – start on page 11
Many families have favorite holiday baking traditions. It's a fund way to get everyone together to make gifts or special holiday meals. We have thirteen suggestions for things to create in the kitchen this year – from pancakes with a holiday theme to sugar cookies and homemade trail mix. Use your own recipes or the links we've provided.

Activities In the Community – start on page 14
While this journal may be about family bonding, there are plenty of things you can do out in the community to build connections at home. These twelve ideas range from going to a tree lighting ceremony in your local community to taking a full-blown trip to a Christmas theme park.

Making Family Traditions – start on page 17
The bulk of the activities in the journal are about making new, and celebrating existing, family traditions. These thirty activities will have you laughing as you plan and celebrate together . Ideas include creating a Family Facebook Page, making an embroidered heirloom table cloth, singing Christmas songs together, and proudly wearing Ugly Sweaters,. With 26 more ideas you'll never run out of Christmas cheer.

The Reason for the Season – start on page 21
It can be easy to get caught up in the commercialism of the season and forget to celebrate the true meaning. Use these thirteen activity ideas to start daily devotionals, have a season of stories, create a traveling nativity in your home, any many more. These thoughtful ideas all center on Christ, the reason for the season.

Activity Planning and Journal Pages - start on page 24

Crafty Ideas

Crafty Ideas

- **Announce the season** - hang a festive wreath on the front door. There are as many wreath ideas as there are people in the world! Do a Google search for "handmade wreath ideas" and choose one of those round-up articles that have at least 50 ideas. You are sure to find the perfect idea that fits your experience level and budget.

- **Make a wreath from fresh materials** - pine boughs, pine cones, berries, etc. Get easy instructions for an Evergreen Wreath at Learning and Yearning.
  https://learningandyearning.com/evergreen-christmas-wreath/

- **Doors aren't just for wreaths!** Try a pair of vintage ice skates packed with fresh greenery from around your yard. Bonus: you can leave it up through February without the neighbors talking!

- **Make paper snowflakes**
  from toilet paper rolls https://www.countryliving.com/diy-crafts/how-to/a6330/diy-toilet-paper-roll-snowflakes/
  Coffee filters https://mom.com/momlife/10231-diy-coffee-filter-snowflakes/ or even snowflake window clings make from white glue
  https://www.firstpalette.com/craft/snowflake-window-clings.html

- **Make a tree ornament.** There are about a bazillion ideas on the internet. We liked these Tea Light Snowmen https://onelittleproject.com/tea-light-snowman-ornaments/2/
  Pine Cone Owl ornaments https://liagriffith.com/felt-pine-cone-owl-ornaments/
  Wine Cork Angels https://onelittleproject.com/wine-cork-angels/
  and pop cycle sleds https://www.cleanandscentsible.com/handmade-christmas-ornaments-popsicle-stick-sleds/

- **Emphasize handmade gifts** this year by making DIY gift baskets. Some ideas include a bread basket, fresh potted herbs, homemade spice seasoning mixes, or homemade jams.

- **Create your own snow globe**. It's quick, it's pretty easy and the kids love it. Teach the kids how to make a snow globe and let them make one of their own!
  https://crazylittleprojects.com/diy-snow-globes-for-kids/

- **Make cinnamon applesauce ornaments**. Use cookie cutters to make stars, trees, or gingerbread men. These will keep their delicious smell for many years.
  https://lovelylittlekitchen.com/cinnamon-applesauce-ornaments/

- **Make handmade Christmas Cards.**
  Try a pop-up card https://www.redtedart.com/diy-christmas-pop-up-card/
  or Paint Chip cards https://onelittleproject.com/paint-chip-christmas-cards

Crafty Ideas

- **Make handmade gift wrapping paper** from butcher paper and tempera paint. Everyone will have a ball creating their own unique look. Use handmade stamps to turn the fun up a notch! https://www.artbarblog.com/diy-wrapping-paper/

- **Make Wooden Nativity Statues.** These cute decorations are made of simple wooden cutouts, easily painted and put together with hot glue. Get directions at https://sugarbeecrafts.com/wooden-nativity-silhouette-statue

- **Make a folded book Christmas tree.** Take an old paperback book from a thrift store and make a cute decoration. It needs to be at least 300 pages in length. Even youngsters can do this project! https://www.itsalwaysautumn.com/folded-book-christmas-tree.html

- **Make a gingerbread house** from Graham Crackers https://www.wikihow.com/Make-Gingerbread-Houses-Using-Graham-Crackers

- **Decorate the tree in a different way.** Instead of using the same old ornaments, try a themed tree this year. Customize your tree to showcase a favorite family hobby or activity, or go for a non-traditional Christmas color.

- **Make a paper chain ring countdown** Children can assemble their own easy holiday paper chain countdown to hang in the home. This advent calendar is made from construction paper and is candy-free. Remove a ring for each day for the Christmas countdown.

- **Make or buy an ornament specific to this year** and start building a collection. Pop popcorn the old-fashioned way https://www.acouplecooks.com/stove-top-popcorn/ and string it with cranberries for the Christmas tree. https://littlecooksreadingbooks.com/how-to-make-popcorn-garland/

- **Make a Christmas centerpiece.** Placing a small pillar vessel inside a larger clear vase, and fill the gaps between the two with colorful, seasonal items. (think red and white marbles, greens, or old ornaments). Next, fill the inner container with a mix of flowers and evergreen sprigs.

- **Make salt dough ornaments.** These will keep for years if properly stored, plus you only need four ingredients (which you already have at home!) to make this fun craft. Don't be fooled - salt dough ornaments aren't just for toddlers. Search online for ideas or try this: https://www.messylittlemonster.com/2014/12/how-to-make-salt-dough-printable-recipe.html

Ways to Give

Ways to Give

- Organize your friends and family and **go Christmas caroling** at a nursing home. Kids love to sing and the residents will appreciate the good cheer and chance to visit with children.

- **Call someone** in your extended family, church organization, or neighborhood who is lonely and brighten their day.

- **Sponsor a family in need** and donate time, talent, or treasure, it all makes a difference! Check with your pastor to see if there is a family in your congregation that is in need. If not, the people at https://www.volunteermatch.org/ can give suggestions.

- **Send a care package** to someone overseas in the military. Start by using the contacts at Anysoldier.com. Basically, it works like this: (1) Select your service branch (2) Look at the contact list for a profile that sparks your interest (3) Request the mail address of that contact (4) Fill up a box and send it off with the "Attn: Any Soldier" in the address. From there, your "contact" will receive the box and distribute it to someone in their unit or command who could use some cheering up. This might be the easiest way to fill a box yourself. Plus, AnySoldier is a registered non-profit run by a military family.

- **Be a secret Santa** to someone at school, work, or in the neighborhood. Do this over several days, so they are surprised several times. Seek out a family or person in need of help this holiday season. Determine their needs and provide help without them having any clue of where it came from. Perhaps a rent payment made in stealth or a prepaid credit card left in a secure location?

- Give back, **work at a food bank** during the season. In spite of the busy season, many people across the country pledge to volunteer at their local soup kitchens, food pantries, and food banks. Find a local food bank
https://www.feedingamerica.org/find-your-local-foodbank

- **Make Christmas cards** for kids teachers. Use some of the ideas in the crafty section to make a special card for your favorite teacher.

Ways to Give

- **Clean closets, playrooms**, etc., and donate old stuff to those in need. The holidays are a great time for kids to donate some of the games, clothing, or other things they own – and clean out some clutter while you're at it. Even preschoolers can pick a few lightly-used toys to donate to kids who don't have any. As an alternative, take kids shopping for new toys they'd love but will donate to a local shelter or nonprofit.

- **Give a surprise gift of service to each member of your family.** Giving an unexpected gift of service to members of your family demonstrates Christ-like love and service. You might consider giving a back rub to your spouse, running an errand for your brother, or cleaning out a closet for your mother. Make it personal and meaningful and watch the blessings multiply.

- **Write a Christmas letter to a missionary.** Many missionaries are unable to travel home for the holidays, so Christmas can be a very lonely time for them. Write a special letter to a missionary of your choice and thank them for giving their life in service to the Lord. It will mean more than you can imagine.

- **Remember the grieving**. Do you know anyone that has lost somebody close to them this Christmas? A death close to Christmas time can be especially difficult, as families or lone individuals struggle to come to terms with the new family dynamics they will be facing this Christmas day. A letter or a phone call to let the grieving know that you are thinking of them and are there for them may really make a difference.

- **Invite Someone to Christmas Dinner**. Depression and feelings of desperate loneliness are very common during the holiday season. We all know people who are spending the season alone. Invite them into your home for Christmas dinner and share the blessings of love and peace.

- **Help furry friends by making homemade dog biscuits** or toys for shelter dogs. For treats, try a seasonal variety, such as Rachael Ray's "Pumpkin" dog treats, which require only four ingredients and 40 minutes. Toys can be made simply by braiding socks (new ones!) or T-shirts.

Ways to Give

- **Make crochet or loom hats** from leftover yarn, then deliver them to a homeless shelter. Find a tutorial at https://thecrochetcrowd.com/loom-knitting-adult-ribbed-hat-pattern/

- **Make Christmas treats and visit house-bound neighbors.** Do you have any neighbors, family members, or friends who can't get around well? Bake some holiday treats for them and invite your children to help you deliver the goodies. Spend the afternoon or evening with them playing cards or games or just simply visiting with one another. Also, see if they need help with anything that your kids can do for them.

- **Send a Letter to a Solider.** Through https://amillionthanks.org/ Our soldiers do so much to keep us safe, which typically means extended stays away from their loved ones. Write them a letter thanking them for their sacrifice and let them know their service is appreciated. A Million Thanks is a great organization to send your letter to a soldier overseas or to grant the wish of an injured veteran.

- **Collect Food for Your Local Food Pantry.** Food pantries often have greater demand than products and Christmas is an especially busy time for them. Call your local pantry and see what items are most needed. Consider hosting or arranging a food drive at your place of worship, workplace, or neighborhood to help replenish their shelves in time for the holidays.

- **Thank The Emergency Services Workers** in your neighborhood. Remember, not everybody gets Christmas day off with their family and friends. Show your appreciation with Christmas cards, cakes, or small treats for your local fire station, police station, or hospital. Bring Christmas to those that are keeping you safe this Christmas!

Joy to the world

In the Kitchen

In the Kitchen

joy · love · peace · believe

- ❏ **Make and drink hot chocolate** as a family. Have a hot cocoa bar and get specialty items to add to your drink besides marshmallows. Try these recipes from -
Taste of Home : https://www.tasteofhome.com/collection/10-creative-mix-ins-for-the-best-hot-chocolate/
Yuppie Chef : https://www.yuppiechef.com/spatula/27-delicious-hot-chocolate-recipes/ or
Spoon University : https://spoonuniversity.com/recipe/25-hot-cocoa-mix-ins-to-get-you-in-the-christmas-spirit

- ❏ **Bake and deliver chocolate chip cookies** to your favorite neighbors. Give them a holiday wrapping and deliver with a carol or homemade gift tag.

- ❏ **Make cookies in a jar and give them as a gift**. Cookie mix in a jar is a particularly fun gift for children (not to mention a convenient one for adults). The process of making cookies has thrilled children for ages, and the rewards of the process—well, they make it all worth it!
https://www.stonefamilyfarmstead.com/cookies-in-a-jar-recipes/

- ❏ **Make hot chocolate bombs.** These are spheres of tempered chocolate filled with hot cocoa mix, mini marshmallows, and other delights. The possibilities are endless. When added to hot milk, the chocolate spheres melt, releasing the cocoa mix and creating a tasty cup of hot chocolate. https://southern-bytes.com/hot-chocolate-bombs/

- ❏ **Create your own Christmas 'trail mix'** and give it to family and friends. Try searching for terms like "white chocolate chex mix", "muddy buddies", "holiday trail mix", or "savory Christmas snack mix". You'll get more ideas than you have time to make and eat.

In the Kitchen

- **Make DIY Hot Cocoa Mix** and give it as a gift. While it's dreamy to make a fresh cup of hot chocolate for the family as a special treat, we know you're busy. Stock your pantry with easy and healthy options for your family and gifts. https://www.thepurposefulpantry.com/diy-hot-cocoa-mix/

- **Make Christmas-themed pancakes** or breakfast. These are so tasty and sure to make a great tradition! For the adults add traditional holiday flavors to your pancakes. How about gingerbread, pumpkin, pecan apple, or cranberry orange? Kids will enjoy pancake snowmen or Santa pancakes with plenty of whipping cream for his beard. https://www.tasteofhome.com/collection/12-days-of-pancakes/

- **Bake Cinnamon Pull aparts** (aka Monkey Bread) for Christmas morning. You can make your own dough or purchase and repurpose biscuit dough.

- **Bake and decorate sugar cookies**. These timeless classics can be rolled out and cut into holiday shapes, then decorated, or rolled into balls and cooked like regular cookies.

- **Make fudge** using your favorite family recipe. Don't have a family recipe yet? Have a fudge cookoff and find the perfect recipe to create a new tradition.

- Learn to **make your own eggnog** and try making different flavors. Give pumpkin, vanilla, French toast, cinnamon roll, even gingerbread eggnog a try!

happy holidays

In the Community

In the Community

- **Go for a nighttime walk and enjoy the Christmas lights** in your neighborhood or a nearby one. Create a rating system (most creative, most lights used, best theme) and deliver cookies to the houses that win.

- **Attend a Christmas play** or pageant in your community.

- **Go to a Christmas Tree lighting** ceremony, where the tree is lit for the first time of the season.

- **Learn about and attend a different Christmas tradition.** Perhaps your family could learn about Hanukkah, the Feast of the Seven Fishes, Kwanzaa, Boxing Day, Saint Nicholas Day, or Ōmisoka.

- **Go to a holiday party** feeling beautiful and wearing your best Christmas clothes.

- **Sit by a bonfire** and make smores (or roast chestnuts) with your neighbors.

- **Go to a theme park, Christmas village, festival**, or someplace that is decorated for Christmas and has activities. Try this link for ideas. https://www.thepioneerwoman.com/holidays-celebrations/g32402603/best-christmas-towns/

- **Do a Christmas scavenger hunt.** You can keep this simple and do it at home or involve the whole neighborhood. Try these links for ideas. https://www.playpartyplan.com/christmas-scavenger-hunt/ or https://www.housebeautiful.com/lifestyle/a29003089/christmas-scavenger-hunt/

- **Hold a neighborhood cookie swap.** Share recipes and ideas and taste the delicious batches of cookies your neighbors have whipped up! You'll come away with some new recipes, a full belly, and holiday cheer!

joy · love · peace · believe

In the Community

- **Play Christmas tree eye spy.** A fun way to get your kids involved on a long car ride (or short!) is to have them play "eye spy" for all the Christmas trees they see in the windows of houses. Keep a running tally of white lights versus colored lights and see what number you have at the end. This also makes a fun neighborhood walking game.

- **Attend a zoo lights activity** at your local zoo. Some are setting up drive-through lights, many are encouraging walking tours, and a few zoos even have train rides to enjoy. Do a search to see which zoo to visit near you.

- **Find a Polar Express Train Ride** near you. Be sure to read the classic book before you go!

- **Take a family drive** to see the neighborhood holiday decorations. Live in a boring neighborhood? Every town seems to have an area known for "putting on the lights" Pile in the car and go on a nighttime tour of your town, decked out in lights and decorations.

joy
love
peace
believe

Family Traditions

Family Traditions

- **Have Christmas movie night** and watch one of the "classics". Some ideas: It's a Wonderful Life, A Christmas Carol, and Miracle on 34th Street, Home Alone 1 or 2, The Santa Clause 1, 2, and 3.

- **Eat a special holiday meal** with your family. Use the best dishes you have and decorate the table for the season.

- **Bring on the lights!** Decorate your yard, living room, or bedroom with Christmas lights.

- **Wrap gifts together.** Use your homemade wrapping paper to liven up under the tree.

- **Start an ornament collection box** for each child. Every year buy a special ornament they can add to their collection. This is something they will take with them when they grow up. Make a big production of the ornament shopping trip. Bundle the kids up in their coats and go out to see the stores all lit up.

- Go out as a family and **cut down your own tree**.

- **Watch Macy's Thanksgiving Day Parade** in person, or on the TV. Make your own categories and vote for things like the best float, best marching band, best balloon, etc.

- **Go to a Christmas bazaar** and support local artisans. You are sure to find inexpensive and unique gifts to give to friends.

- Set up an area for people to **kiss under the mistletoe**. Your littles will love the tradition!

- **Send a family letter to Santa** - Tell him why your family has been naughty or nice.

- **Get a family picture taken with Santa**. Can't get out to see one in person? Have the family choose their favorite picture of Santa and Photoshop him in your last family picture.

Family Traditions

- **Find a way to play in the snow** and have a snowball fight.

- **Go sledding with a twist.** Do sled bowling, have an X-games challenge, or make a sledding obstacle course.. https://www.hisawyer.com/blog/7-fun-games-to-play-sledding

- **Proudly wear an ugly Christmas sweater** - this could be broken into several ideas. Go shopping at a thrift store for ugly sweaters. Bring them home and use yarn, buttons, and ornaments to make them even uglier. Wear them out as a family on National Ugly Christmas Sweater Day, which is the third Friday of December. . Get your picture taken as a family with your ugly sweaters. learn the history of the "ugly sweater" https://www.cnn.com/style/article/ugly-christmas-jumpers/index.html

- **Listen to Christmas music.** Try all kinds - traditional church hymns like Hark the Herald Angels Sing, the Golden Age carols from Bing Crosby, Nat King Cole, and Andy Williams, country Christmas tunes, or the recent pop covers. Don't forget to add in trusty songs like Frosty the Snowman and Jingle Bell Rock!

- **Create a family holiday Facebook page** and invite your relatives to see what you have going on this holiday season. You could post each of the activities you experienced for your 31 days of Christmas celebrations.

- **Write a letter updating** everything that's been going on with your family the past year and send old-fashioned Christmas cards.

- **Read a treasured Christmas book** aloud as a family. Try The Gift of the Magi by O. Henry or A Christmas Carol by Charles Dickens. Taking a road trip? Use Audible and listen to them while you drive.

- **Do a secret Santa gift exchange** with your family members. Set some rules about the amount of money that can be spent and whether the gift needs to be purchased or homemade.

- **Have a family game night.** From Hallmark Channel movie bingo that'll put your family's Christmas-movie knowledge to the test and Pictionary to charades games that reference Christmas songs, there's something here for everyone. https://www.countryliving.com/life/g23477105/family-christmas-games

- **Bring out the special Christmas mugs!** Do you have mugs that only get used for the holiday season? Start a family tradition and have hot cocoa every night - but only when the holiday mugs are out.

Family Traditions

- **Wear matching Christmas pajamas** and be sure to take a picture!

- **Go ice skating** at a local rink.

- **Brave the crowds** and go shopping on Black Friday!

- **Start or continue a Christmas Eve tradition.** Drink special hot chocolate, give everyone new PJ's, visit relatives, or open your presents early.

- **Set up cookies and milk for Santa.** Worried that Santa needs to lose weight or is wheat sensitive? Make keto or gluten-free cookies this year.

- **Make an Embroidered Heirloom Tablecloth.** Heirloom treasures are one of the most precious things that can be passed down the family line, especially when family members are represented through the years. Start by having your family members sign a tablecloth during the get-together this year. Then after everyone leaves embroider their names. This tablecloth can be made and used during the holidays and will serve as a precious memory of past holiday gatherings. https://www.stonefamilyfarmstead.com/embroidered-heirloom-tablecloth/

- **Hang a gratitude banner.** Make a banner from butcher paper or wrapping paper that can be written on, and tack it to a wall that everyone can see. Each day in December, ask family members to list the things they are thankful for. Ask anyone that visits to contribute too. Spend some time on Christmas eve looking at all the reasons your family has to be grateful.

- **Hang a stocking for a family member** who has passed away the previous year. Perhaps you have a beloved grandmother or grandfather that died this past year. Hang a stocking to help family members honor their life. As you think of them, put in love notes and cherished memories inside. This is a great way to help kids with their grief and work through their feelings of loss.

- **Put out a Christmas-themed puzzle** for the family to finish during downtimes. You'll find that all guests will take a try at it during holiday gatherings. Consider 300 piece puzzles for the kids and 1000 pieces for the experienced. Challenge them to finish the puzzle on Christmas day!

- **Make a "Night Before Christmas Box"** for each child. This gives them something to open and can become a special family tradition. Items might include pajamas, a Christmas book, a stuffed animal, and a small snack. Get ideas with this link. https://thewhoot.com/whoot-news/crafty-corner/night-before-christmas-box

The Reason for the Season

The Reason for the Season

- ❑ **Read the story of the birth of Jesus** as a family. Find it in Matthew 1:18-25 and Luke 2:1-14. The visit of the shepherds can be found in Luke 2:15-20

- ❑ Draw pictures to **illustrate the story of the Birth of Jesus**. Use them as park of your holiday decorations.

- ❑ **Make "The Names of Jesus" ornaments** for your tree. One year we spent an hour looking up all the names for Jesus we could find in the scriptures. (Counselor, Wonderful, Prince of Peace, etc.) and then we made simple star ornaments with those names written on them. This was a thoughtful way to bring the reason for the season to our usual "commercially" minded Christmas tree. https://www.crosswalk.com/blogs/debbie-mcdaniel/50-names-of-jesus-who-the-bible-says-christ-is.html

- ❑ **Sing in a Christmas Choir,** or attend a Christmas Concert at your place of worship.

- ❑ **Have a traveling nativity in your home**. Move the Wise Men, and Mary and Joseph closer to the manger each day. Mary and Joseph arrive on December 24th, the Wise Men arrive on January 6th. The kids will have fun moving them around and anticipating their arrival.

- ❑ **Extend the season and celebrate Epiphany.** It is celebrated 12 days after Christmas, on 6 January, and commemorates the visit of the wise men to the infant Jesus. Epiphany literally means 'revealed', and this day also marks the day when Jesus was revealed to the world. The Visit of the Wise Men is in Matthew 2:1-15

Merry Christmas

The Reason for the Season

joy • love • peace • believe

- **Visit a live nativity display in your community.** From marketplaces to beggars and singing angels, live animals, and a stand-in Baby Jesus, live nativities bring this very real story to life right in front of your eyes. It is an especially neat experience for younger children to visualize the events surrounding Christ's birth as real, actual events.

- **Attend a candlelight church service** with family and friends.

- **Invite someone to worship with you.** Christmas is about the birth of man's salvation and the hope of eternal life in the presence of God. That is the true gift of this season and it is everlasting. Share it as we are commanded to do, by spreading this good news and inviting others to receive it too.

- **Have a daily devotional.** Reading a devotional each day with your family during the countdown to Christmas is a fantastic way to set the mood for purposeful giving. There are many sources to choose from, and they can be found online.

- **Have a season of stories.** Find books about Christmas in local thrift shops and garage sales, search for books that tell the Christmas story from different perspectives, and demonstrate the true spirit of the season. Wrap each book individually, and starting on Dec. 1, select one book to read each night as a family. This tradition helps you wind down each evening with a focus on Christ and the celebration of His birth.

- **The Gift of Scripture.** Ask each family member to select a scripture that has meant something to them during the course of the year. On Christmas morning, take turns reading your chosen verse or passage and share why it was important to you. This is a thoughtful way to include Jesus in the gift-giving, and it helps everyone grow a little closer to our Savior.

Activity #1

Where is this activity taking place?

Address:

Activity date:

starts at time:

Need reservations for this activity? Y N
We made them for
date:
time:
phone:

Lodging:
Address:

Reservations? Y N
For date

The plan for the activity:

This is what you will be doing. List the details of the activity
_____
_____
_____
_____
_____
_____
_____

What is the hoped for outcome? What do you hope to feel / learn as a family during this activity?
_____
_____
_____

Supplies needed

_____
_____
_____
_____
_____
_____

Budget for this activity:

Food	$
Supplies	$
Entrance Fee	$
Parking / Gas	$
Lodging	$
Tour / Rental	$
Total	$

Describe the activity. Who was there, did you stick to the plan or improvise? How?
_____
_____
_____
_____
_____

Was this a good family bonding activity? How did it get you in the Christmas spirit?
_____
_____

What was the funniest moment at this activity?
_____
_____

What surprised you the most about this activity?
_____
_____

Was there something disappointing? Could the day could have been better? How would you change it?
_____
_____

When you look back at it, what kinds of feelings will you associate with this activity?
_____
_____

What do you want your child(ren) to remember most about this activity?
_____
_____

What is one thing about today you never want to forget?
_____
_____

Rate this activity on a scale of 1-5. Why did you give it this rating?
_____

Activity #2

Where is this activity taking place?

Address:

Activity date:

starts at time:

Need reservations for this activity? Y   N
We made them for
date:
time:
phone:

Lodging:
Address:

Reservations? Y   N
For date

The plan for the activity:

This is what you will be doing. List the details of the activity

_____
_____
_____
_____
_____
_____
_____

What is the hoped for outcome? What do you hope to feel / learn as a family during this activity?

_____
_____
_____

Supplies needed

_____
_____
_____
_____
_____
_____

Budget for this activity:

Food	$
Supplies	$
Entrance Fee	$
Parking / Gas	$
Lodging	$
Tour / Rental	$
Total	$

Describe the activity. Who was there, did you stick to the plan or improvise? How?

Was this a good family bonding activity? How did it get you in the Christmas spirit?

What was the funniest moment at this activity?

What surprised you the most about this activity?

Was there something disappointing? Could the day could have been better? How would you change it?

When you look back at it, what kinds of feelings will you associate with this activity?

What do you want your child(ren) to remember most about this activity?

What is one thing about today you never want to forget?

Rate this activity on a scale of 1-5. Why did you give it this rating?

Activity #3

Where is this activity taking place?

Address:

Activity date:

starts at time:

Need reservations for this activity? Y   N

We made them for

date:

time:

phone:

Lodging:

Address:

Reservations? Y   N

For date

The plan for the activity:

This is what you will be doing. List the details of the activity
_____
_____
_____
_____
_____
_____
_____

What is the hoped for outcome? What do you hope to feel / learn as a family during this activity?
_____
_____
_____

Supplies needed

_____
_____
_____
_____
_____
_____
_____

Budget for this activity:

Food	$
Supplies	$
Entrance Fee	$
Parking / Gas	$
Lodging	$
Tour / Rental	$
Total	$

Describe the activity. Who was there, did you stick to the plan or improvise? How?

Was this a good family bonding activity? How did it get you in the Christmas spirit?

What was the funniest moment at this activity?

What surprised you the most about this activity?

Was there something disappointing? Could the day could have been better? How would you change it?

When you look back at it, what kinds of feelings will you associate with this activity?

What do you want your child(ren) to remember most about this activity?

What is one thing about today you never want to forget?

Rate this activity on a scale of 1-5. Why did you give it this rating?

Activity #4

Where is this activity taking place?

Address:

Activity date:

starts at time:

Need reservations for this activity? Y N
We made them for
date:
time:
phone:

Lodging:
Address:

Reservations? Y   N
For date

The plan for the activity:

This is what you will be doing. List the details of the activity
___
___
___
___
___
___
___
___

What is the hoped for outcome? What do you hope to feel / learn as a family during this activity?
___
___
___

Supplies needed

___
___
___
___
___
___

Budget for this activity:

Food	$
Supplies	$
Entrance Fee	$
Parking / Gas	$
Lodging	$
Tour / Rental	$
Total	$

Describe the activity. Who was there, did you stick to the plan or improvise? How?

___

Was this a good family bonding activity? How did it get you in the Christmas spirit?

___

What was the funniest moment at this activity?

___

What surprised you the most about this activity?

___

Was there something disappointing? Could the day could have been better? How would you change it?

___

When you look back at it, what kinds of feelings will you associate with this activity?

___

What do you want your child(ren) to remember most about this activity?

___

What is one thing about today you never want to forget?

___

Rate this activity on a scale of 1-5. Why did you give it this rating?

Activity #5

Where is this activity taking place?

Address:

Activity date:

starts at time:

Need reservations for this activity? Y   N

We made them for
date:
time:
phone:

Lodging:

Address:

Reservations? Y   N

For date

The plan for the activity:

This is what you will be doing. List the details of the activity

_____
_____
_____
_____
_____
_____
_____
_____

What is the hoped for outcome? What do you hope to feel / learn as a family during this activity?

_____
_____
_____

Supplies needed

_____
_____
_____
_____
_____
_____
_____

Budget for this activity:

Food	$
Supplies	$
Entrance Fee	$
Parking / Gas	$
Lodging	$
Tour / Rental	$
Total	$

Describe the activity. Who was there, did you stick to the plan or improvise? How?

Was this a good family bonding activity? How did it get you in the Christmas spirit?

What was the funniest moment at this activity?

What surprised you the most about this activity?

Was there something disappointing? Could the day could have been better? How would you change it?

When you look back at it, what kinds of feelings will you associate with this activity?

What do you want your child(ren) to remember most about this activity?

What is one thing about today you never want to forget?

Rate this activity on a scale of 1-5. Why did you give it this rating?

Activity #6

Where is this activity taking place?

Address:

Activity date:

starts at time:

Need reservations for this activity? Y N
We made them for
date:
time:
phone:

Lodging:
Address:

Reservations? Y N
For date

The plan for the activity:

This is what you will be doing. List the details of the activity

_____
_____
_____
_____
_____
_____
_____

What is the hoped for outcome? What do you hope to feel / learn as a family during this activity?

_____
_____
_____

Supplies needed

_____
_____
_____
_____
_____
_____

Budget for this activity:

Food	$
Supplies	$
Entrance Fee	$
Parking / Gas	$
Lodging	$
Tour / Rental	$
Total	$

Describe the activity. Who was there, did you stick to the plan or improvise? How?

___

Was this a good family bonding activity? How did it get you in the Christmas spirit?

___

What was the funniest moment at this activity?

___

What surprised you the most about this activity?

___

Was there something disappointing? Could the day could have been better? How would you change it?

___

When you look back at it, what kinds of feelings will you associate with this activity?

___

What do you want your child(ren) to remember most about this activity?

___

What is one thing about today you never want to forget?

___

Rate this activity on a scale of 1-5. Why did you give it this rating?

Activity #7

Where is this activity taking place?

Address:

Activity date:

starts at time:

Need reservations for this activity? Y N
We made them for
date:
time:
phone:

Lodging:
Address:

Reservations? Y N
For date

The plan for the activity:

This is what you will be doing. List the details of the activity
_____
_____
_____
_____
_____
_____
_____

What is the hoped for outcome? What do you hope to feel / learn as a family during this activity?
_____
_____
_____

Supplies needed

_____
_____
_____
_____
_____
_____

Budget for this activity:

Food	$
Supplies	$
Entrance Fee	$
Parking / Gas	$
Lodging	$
Tour / Rental	$
Total	$

Describe the activity. Who was there, did you stick to the plan or improvise? How?

_____
_____
_____
_____
_____

Was this a good family bonding activity? How did it get you in the Christmas spirit?

_____
_____

What was the funniest moment at this activity?

_____
_____

What surprised you the most about this activity?

_____
_____

Was there something disappointing? Could the day could have been better? How would you change it?

_____
_____

When you look back at it, what kinds of feelings will you associate with this activity?

_____
_____

What do you want your child(ren) to remember most about this activity?

_____
_____

What is one thing about today you never want to forget?

_____
_____

Rate this activity on a scale of 1-5. Why did you give it this rating?

_____

Activity #8

Where is this activity taking place?

Address:

Activity date:

starts at time:

Need reservations for this activity? Y N
We made them for
date:
time:
phone:

Lodging:
Address:

Reservations? Y N
For date

The plan for the activity:

This is what you will be doing. List the details of the activity
_____
_____
_____
_____
_____
_____
_____

What is the hoped for outcome? What do you hope to feel / learn as a family during this activity?
_____
_____
_____

Supplies needed

_____
_____
_____
_____
_____
_____

Budget for this activity:

Food	$
Supplies	$
Entrance Fee	$
Parking / Gas	$
Lodging	$
Tour / Rental	$
Total	$

Describe the activity. Who was there, did you stick to the plan or improvise? How?

Was this a good family bonding activity? How did it get you in the Christmas spirit?

What was the funniest moment at this activity?

What surprised you the most about this activity?

Was there something disappointing? Could the day could have been better? How would you change it?

When you look back at it, what kinds of feelings will you associate with this activity?

What do you want your child(ren) to remember most about this activity?

What is one thing about today you never want to forget?

Rate this activity on a scale of 1-5. Why did you give it this rating?

Activity #9

Where is this activity taking place?

Address:

Activity date:

starts at time:

Need reservations for this activity? Y N

We made them for
date:
time:
phone:

Lodging:

Address:

Reservations? Y N

For date

The plan for the activity:

This is what you will be doing. List the details of the activity

_____
_____
_____
_____
_____
_____
_____

What is the hoped for outcome? What do you hope to feel / learn as a family during this activity?

_____
_____
_____

Supplies needed

_____
_____
_____
_____
_____
_____
_____

Budget for this activity:

Food	$
Supplies	$
Entrance Fee	$
Parking / Gas	$
Lodging	$
Tour / Rental	$
Total	$

Describe the activity. Who was there, did you stick to the plan or improvise? How?

___
___
___
___
___
___

Was this a good family bonding activity? How did it get you in the Christmas spirit?

___
___
___

What was the funniest moment at this activity?

___
___
___

What surprised you the most about this activity?

___
___
___

Was there something disappointing? Could the day could have been better? How would you change it?

___
___
___

When you look back at it, what kinds of feelings will you associate with this activity?

___
___
___

What do you want your child(ren) to remember most about this activity?

___
___
___

What is one thing about today you never want to forget?

___
___
___

Rate this activity on a scale of 1-5. Why did you give it this rating?

___

Activity #10

Where is this activity taking place?

Address:

Activity date:

starts at time:

Need reservations for this activity? Y N
We made them for
date:
time:
phone:

Lodging:
Address:

Reservations? Y N
For date

The plan for the activity:

This is what you will be doing. List the details of the activity

_____
_____
_____
_____
_____
_____
_____
_____

What is the hoped for outcome? What do you hope to feel / learn as a family during this activity?

_____
_____
_____

Supplies needed

_____
_____
_____
_____
_____
_____

Budget for this activity:

Food	$
Supplies	$
Entrance Fee	$
Parking / Gas	$
Lodging	$
Tour / Rental	$
Total	$

Describe the activity. Who was there, did you stick to the plan or improvise? How?

_____
_____
_____
_____
_____

Was this a good family bonding activity? How did it get you in the Christmas spirit?

_____
_____

What was the funniest moment at this activity?

_____
_____

What surprised you the most about this activity?

_____
_____

Was there something disappointing? Could the day could have been better? How would you change it?

_____
_____

When you look back at it, what kinds of feelings will you associate with this activity?

_____
_____

What do you want your child(ren) to remember most about this activity?

_____
_____

What is one thing about today you never want to forget?

_____
_____

Rate this activity on a scale of 1-5. Why did you give it this rating?

_____

Activity #11

Where is this activity taking place?

Address:

Activity date:

starts at time:

Need reservations for this activity? Y N

We made them for
date:
time:
phone:

Lodging:

Address:

Reservations? Y N

For date

The plan for the activity:

This is what you will be doing. List the details of the activity
_____
_____
_____
_____
_____
_____
_____

What is the hoped for outcome? What do you hope to feel / learn as a family during this activity?
_____
_____
_____

Supplies needed

_____
_____
_____
_____
_____
_____

Budget for this activity:

Food	$
Supplies	$
Entrance Fee	$
Parking / Gas	$
Lodging	$
Tour / Rental	$
Total	$

Describe the activity. Who was there, did you stick to the plan or improvise? How?
_____
_____
_____
_____
_____

Was this a good family bonding activity? How did it get you in the Christmas spirit?
_____
_____

What was the funniest moment at this activity?
_____
_____

What surprised you the most about this activity?
_____
_____

Was there something disappointing? Could the day could have been better? How would you change it?
_____
_____

When you look back at it, what kinds of feelings will you associate with this activity?
_____
_____

What do you want your child(ren) to remember most about this activity?
_____
_____

What is one thing about today you never want to forget?
_____
_____

Rate this activity on a scale of 1-5. Why did you give it this rating?
_____

Activity #12

Where is this activity taking place?

Address:

Activity date:

starts at time:

Need reservations for this activity? Y   N
We made them for
date:
time:
phone:

Lodging:
Address:

Reservations? Y   N
For date

The plan for the activity:

This is what you will be doing. List the details of the activity
_____
_____
_____
_____
_____
_____
_____

What is the hoped for outcome? What do you hope to feel / learn as a family during this activity?
_____
_____
_____

Supplies needed

_____
_____
_____
_____
_____
_____

Budget for this activity:

Food	$
Supplies	$
Entrance Fee	$
Parking / Gas	$
Lodging	$
Tour / Rental	$
Total	$

Describe the activity. Who was there, did you stick to the plan or improvise? How?

_____
_____
_____
_____
_____

Was this a good family bonding activity? How did it get you in the Christmas spirit?

_____
_____

What was the funniest moment at this activity?

_____
_____

What surprised you the most about this activity?

_____
_____

Was there something disappointing? Could the day could have been better? How would you change it?

_____
_____

When you look back at it, what kinds of feelings will you associate with this activity?

_____
_____

What do you want your child(ren) to remember most about this activity?

_____
_____

What is one thing about today you never want to forget?

_____
_____

Rate this activity on a scale of 1-5. Why did you give it this rating?

_____

Activity #13

Where is this activity taking place?

Address:

Activity date:

starts at time:

Need reservations for this activity? Y   N
We made them for
date:
time:
phone:

Lodging:

Address:

Reservations? Y   N
For date

The plan for the activity:

This is what you will be doing. List the details of the activity

_____
_____
_____
_____
_____
_____
_____
_____

What is the hoped for outcome? What do you hope to feel / learn as a family during this activity?

_____
_____
_____

Supplies needed

_____
_____
_____
_____
_____
_____

Budget for this activity:

Food	$
Supplies	$
Entrance Fee	$
Parking / Gas	$
Lodging	$
Tour / Rental	$
Total	$

Describe the activity. Who was there, did you stick to the plan or improvise? How?

_____
_____
_____
_____
_____
_____

Was this a good family bonding activity? How did it get you in the Christmas spirit?

_____
_____
_____

What was the funniest moment at this activity?

_____
_____

What surprised you the most about this activity?

_____
_____

Was there something disappointing? Could the day could have been better? How would you change it?

_____
_____
_____

When you look back at it, what kinds of feelings will you associate with this activity?

_____
_____

What do you want your child(ren) to remember most about this activity?

_____
_____

What is one thing about today you never want to forget?

_____
_____

Rate this activity on a scale of 1-5. Why did you give it this rating?

Activity #14

Where is this activity taking place?

Address:

Activity date:

starts at time:

Need reservations for this activity? Y N
We made them for
date:
time:
phone:

Lodging:
Address:

Reservations? Y N
For date

The plan for the activity:

This is what you will be doing. List the details of the activity

_____
_____
_____
_____
_____
_____
_____

What is the hoped for outcome? What do you hope to feel / learn as a family during this activity?

_____
_____
_____

Supplies needed

_____
_____
_____
_____
_____
_____

Budget for this activity:

Food	$
Supplies	$
Entrance Fee	$
Parking / Gas	$
Lodging	$
Tour / Rental	$
Total	$

Describe the activity. Who was there, did you stick to the plan or improvise? How?

___

Was this a good family bonding activity? How did it get you in the Christmas spirit?

___

What was the funniest moment at this activity?

___

What surprised you the most about this activity?

___

Was there something disappointing? Could the day could have been better? How would you change it?

___

When you look back at it, what kinds of feelings will you associate with this activity?

___

What do you want your child(ren) to remember most about this activity?

___

What is one thing about today you never want to forget?

___

Rate this activity on a scale of 1-5. Why did you give it this rating?

Activity #15

Where is this activity taking place?

Address:

Activity date:

starts at time:

Need reservations for this activity? Y   N

We made them for

date:

time:

phone:

Lodging:

Address:

Reservations? Y   N

For date

The plan for the activity:

This is what you will be doing. List the details of the activity
_____
_____
_____
_____
_____
_____
_____
_____

What is the hoped for outcome? What do you hope to feel / learn as a family during this activity?
_____
_____
_____

Supplies needed

_____
_____
_____
_____
_____
_____

Budget for this activity:

Food	$
Supplies	$
Entrance Fee	$
Parking / Gas	$
Lodging	$
Tour / Rental	$
Total	$

Describe the activity. Who was there, did you stick to the plan or improvise? How?

Was this a good family bonding activity? How did it get you in the Christmas spirit?

What was the funniest moment at this activity?

What surprised you the most about this activity?

Was there something disappointing? Could the day could have been better? How would you change it?

When you look back at it, what kinds of feelings will you associate with this activity?

What do you want your child(ren) to remember most about this activity?

What is one thing about today you never want to forget?

Rate this activity on a scale of 1-5. Why did you give it this rating?

Activity #16

Where is this activity taking place?

Address:

Activity date:

starts at time:

Need reservations for this activity? Y N
We made them for
date:
time:
phone:

Lodging:
Address:

Reservations? Y   N
For date

The plan for the activity:

This is what you will be doing. List the details of the activity
_____
_____
_____
_____
_____
_____
_____

What is the hoped for outcome? What do you hope to feel / learn as a family during this activity?
_____
_____
_____

Supplies needed

_____
_____
_____
_____
_____
_____

Budget for this activity:

Food	$
Supplies	$
Entrance Fee	$
Parking / Gas	$
Lodging	$
Tour / Rental	$
Total	$

Describe the activity. Who was there, did you stick to the plan or improvise? How?

Was this a good family bonding activity? How did it get you in the Christmas spirit?

What was the funniest moment at this activity?

What surprised you the most about this activity?

Was there something disappointing? Could the day could have been better? How would you change it?

When you look back at it, what kinds of feelings will you associate with this activity?

What do you want your child(ren) to remember most about this activity?

What is one thing about today you never want to forget?

Rate this activity on a scale of 1-5. Why did you give it this rating?

Activity #17

Where is this activity taking place?

Address:

Activity date:

starts at time:

Need reservations for this activity? Y   N

We made them for
date:
time:
phone:

Lodging:

Address:

Reservations? Y   N

For date

The plan for the activity:

This is what you will be doing. List the details of the activity
_____
_____
_____
_____
_____
_____
_____

What is the hoped for outcome? What do you hope to feel / learn as a family during this activity?
_____
_____
_____

Supplies needed

_____
_____
_____
_____
_____
_____
_____

Budget for this activity:

Food	$
Supplies	$
Entrance Fee	$
Parking / Gas	$
Lodging	$
Tour / Rental	$
Total	$

Describe the activity. Who was there, did you stick to the plan or improvise? How?

Was this a good family bonding activity? How did it get you in the Christmas spirit?

What was the funniest moment at this activity?

What surprised you the most about this activity?

Was there something disappointing? Could the day could have been better? How would you change it?

When you look back at it, what kinds of feelings will you associate with this activity?

What do you want your child(ren) to remember most about this activity?

What is one thing about today you never want to forget?

Rate this activity on a scale of 1-5. Why did you give it this rating?

Activity #18

Where is this activity taking place?

Address:

Activity date:

starts at time:

Need reservations for this activity? Y N
We made them for
date:
time:
phone:

Lodging:
Address:

Reservations? Y N
For date

The plan for the activity:

This is what you will be doing. List the details of the activity
_____
_____
_____
_____
_____
_____
_____
_____

What is the hoped for outcome? What do you hope to feel / learn as a family during this activity?
_____
_____
_____

Supplies needed

_____
_____
_____
_____
_____
_____

Budget for this activity:

Food	$
Supplies	$
Entrance Fee	$
Parking / Gas	$
Lodging	$
Tour / Rental	$
Total	$

Describe the activity. Who was there, did you stick to the plan or improvise? How?

_____
_____
_____
_____
_____

Was this a good family bonding activity? How did it get you in the Christmas spirit?

_____
_____

What was the funniest moment at this activity?

_____
_____

What surprised you the most about this activity?

_____
_____

Was there something disappointing? Could the day could have been better? How would you change it?

_____
_____
_____

When you look back at it, what kinds of feelings will you associate with this activity?

_____
_____

What do you want your child(ren) to remember most about this activity?

_____
_____

What is one thing about today you never want to forget?

_____
_____

Rate this activity on a scale of 1-5. Why did you give it this rating?

Activity #19

Where is this activity taking place?

Address:

Activity date:

starts at time:

Need reservations for this activity? Y   N

We made them for

date:

time:

phone:

Lodging:

Address:

Reservations? Y   N

For date

The plan for the activity:

This is what you will be doing. List the details of the activity

_____
_____
_____
_____
_____
_____
_____

What is the hoped for outcome? What do you hope to feel / learn as a family during this activity?

_____
_____
_____

Supplies needed

_____
_____
_____
_____
_____
_____
_____

Budget for this activity:

Food	$
Supplies	$
Entrance Fee	$
Parking / Gas	$
Lodging	$
Tour / Rental	$
Total	$

Describe the activity. Who was there, did you stick to the plan or improvise? How?

_____
_____
_____
_____
_____
_____

Was this a good family bonding activity? How did it get you in the Christmas spirit?

_____
_____
_____

What was the funniest moment at this activity?

_____
_____

What surprised you the most about this activity?

_____
_____

Was there something disappointing? Could the day could have been better? How would you change it?

_____
_____

When you look back at it, what kinds of feelings will you associate with this activity?

_____
_____

What do you want your child(ren) to remember most about this activity?

_____
_____

What is one thing about today you never want to forget?

_____
_____

Rate this activity on a scale of 1-5. Why did you give it this rating?

_____

Activity #20

Where is this activity taking place?

Address:

Activity date:

starts at time:

Need reservations for this activity? Y   N
We made them for
date:
time:
phone:

Lodging:
Address:

Reservations? Y   N
For date

The plan for the activity:

This is what you will be doing. List the details of the activity

What is the hoped for outcome? What do you hope to feel / learn as a family during this activity?

Supplies needed

Budget for this activity:

Food	$
Supplies	$
Entrance Fee	$
Parking / Gas	$
Lodging	$
Tour / Rental	$
Total	$

Describe the activity. Who was there, did you stick to the plan or improvise? How?

Was this a good family bonding activity? How did it get you in the Christmas spirit?

What was the funniest moment at this activity?

What surprised you the most about this activity?

Was there something disappointing? Could the day could have been better? How would you change it?

When you look back at it, what kinds of feelings will you associate with this activity?

What do you want your child(ren) to remember most about this activity?

What is one thing about today you never want to forget?

Rate this activity on a scale of 1-5. Why did you give it this rating?

Activity #21

Where is this activity taking place?

Address:

Activity date:

starts at time:

Need reservations for this activity? Y N
We made them for
date:
time:
phone:

Lodging:
Address:

Reservations? Y N
For date

The plan for the activity:

This is what you will be doing. List the details of the activity
_____
_____
_____
_____
_____
_____
_____

What is the hoped for outcome? What do you hope to feel / learn as a family during this activity?
_____
_____
_____

Supplies needed

_____
_____
_____
_____
_____
_____

Budget for this activity:

Food	$
Supplies	$
Entrance Fee	$
Parking / Gas	$
Lodging	$
Tour / Rental	$
Total	$

Describe the activity. Who was there, did you stick to the plan or improvise? How?

_____
_____
_____
_____
_____

Was this a good family bonding activity? How did it get you in the Christmas spirit?

_____
_____
_____

What was the funniest moment at this activity?

_____
_____

What surprised you the most about this activity?

_____
_____

Was there something disappointing? Could the day could have been better? How would you change it?

_____
_____
_____

When you look back at it, what kinds of feelings will you associate with this activity?

_____
_____

What do you want your child(ren) to remember most about this activity?

_____
_____
_____

What is one thing about today you never want to forget?

_____
_____

Rate this activity on a scale of 1-5. Why did you give it this rating?
_____

Activity #22

Where is this activity taking place?

Address:

Activity date:

starts at time:

Need reservations for this activity? Y N
We made them for
date:
time:
phone:

Lodging:
Address:

Reservations? Y   N
For date

The plan for the activity:

This is what you will be doing. List the details of the activity

_____
_____
_____
_____
_____
_____
_____

What is the hoped for outcome? What do you hope to feel / learn as a family during this activity?

_____
_____
_____

Supplies needed

_____
_____
_____
_____
_____
_____

Budget for this activity:

Food	$
Supplies	$
Entrance Fee	$
Parking / Gas	$
Lodging	$
Tour / Rental	$
Total	$

Describe the activity. Who was there, did you stick to the plan or improvise? How?
_____
_____
_____
_____
_____

Was this a good family bonding activity? How did it get you in the Christmas spirit?
_____
_____

What was the funniest moment at this activity?
_____
_____

What surprised you the most about this activity?
_____
_____

Was there something disappointing? Could the day could have been better? How would you change it?
_____
_____

When you look back at it, what kinds of feelings will you associate with this activity?
_____
_____

What do you want your child(ren) to remember most about this activity?
_____
_____

What is one thing about today you never want to forget?
_____
_____

Rate this activity on a scale of 1-5. Why did you give it this rating?
_____

Activity #23

Where is this activity taking place?

Address:

Activity date:

starts at time:

Need reservations for this activity?   Y   N

We made them for

date:

time:

phone:

Lodging:

Address:

Reservations?   Y   N

For date

The plan for the activity:

This is what you will be doing. List the details of the activity
_____
_____
_____
_____
_____
_____
_____

What is the hoped for outcome? What do you hope to feel / learn as a family during this activity?
_____
_____
_____

Supplies needed

_____
_____
_____
_____
_____
_____
_____

Budget for this activity:

Food	$
Supplies	$
Entrance Fee	$
Parking / Gas	$
Lodging	$
Tour / Rental	$
Total	$

Describe the activity. Who was there, did you stick to the plan or improvise? How?

Was this a good family bonding activity? How did it get you in the Christmas spirit?

What was the funniest moment at this activity?

What surprised you the most about this activity?

Was there something disappointing? Could the day could have been better? How would you change it?

When you look back at it, what kinds of feelings will you associate with this activity?

What do you want your child(ren) to remember most about this activity?

What is one thing about today you never want to forget?

Rate this activity on a scale of 1-5. Why did you give it this rating?

Activity #24

Where is this activity taking place?

Address:

Activity date:

starts at time:

Need reservations for this activity? Y N
We made them for
date:
time:
phone:

Lodging:
Address:

Reservations? Y   N
For date

The plan for the activity:

This is what you will be doing. List the details of the activity
_____
_____
_____
_____
_____
_____
_____

What is the hoped for outcome? What do you hope to feel / learn as a family during this activity?
_____
_____
_____

Supplies needed

_____
_____
_____
_____
_____
_____

Budget for this activity:

Food	$
Supplies	$
Entrance Fee	$
Parking / Gas	$
Lodging	$
Tour / Rental	$
Total	$

Describe the activity. Who was there, did you stick to the plan or improvise? How?

_____
_____
_____
_____
_____

Was this a good family bonding activity? How did it get you in the Christmas spirit?

_____
_____

What was the funniest moment at this activity?

_____
_____

What surprised you the most about this activity?

_____
_____

Was there something disappointing? Could the day could have been better? How would you change it?

_____
_____

When you look back at it, what kinds of feelings will you associate with this activity?

_____
_____

What do you want your child(ren) to remember most about this activity?

_____
_____

What is one thing about today you never want to forget?

_____
_____

Rate this activity on a scale of 1-5. Why did you give it this rating?

Activity #25

Where is this activity taking place?

Address:

Activity date:

starts at time:

Need reservations for this activity? Y   N
We made them for
date:
time:
phone:

Lodging:
Address:

Reservations? Y   N
For date

The plan for the activity:

This is what you will be doing. List the details of the activity

_____
_____
_____
_____
_____
_____
_____

What is the hoped for outcome? What do you hope to feel / learn as a family during this activity?

_____
_____
_____

Supplies needed

_____
_____
_____
_____
_____
_____
_____

Budget for this activity:

Food	$
Supplies	$
Entrance Fee	$
Parking / Gas	$
Lodging	$
Tour / Rental	$
Total	$

Describe the activity. Who was there, did you stick to the plan or improvise? How?

Was this a good family bonding activity? How did it get you in the Christmas spirit?

What was the funniest moment at this activity?

What surprised you the most about this activity?

Was there something disappointing? Could the day could have been better? How would you change it?

When you look back at it, what kinds of feelings will you associate with this activity?

What do you want your child(ren) to remember most about this activity?

What is one thing about today you never want to forget?

Rate this activity on a scale of 1-5. Why did you give it this rating?

Activity #26

Where is this activity taking place?

Address:

Need reservations for this activity? Y N

We made them for
date:
time:
phone:

Lodging:
Address:

Reservations? Y N
For date

Activity date:

starts at time:

The plan for the activity:

This is what you will be doing. List the details of the activity
_____
_____
_____
_____
_____
_____
_____
_____

What is the hoped for outcome? What do you hope to feel / learn as a family during this activity?
_____
_____
_____

Supplies needed

_____
_____
_____
_____
_____
_____

Budget for this activity:

Food	$
Supplies	$
Entrance Fee	$
Parking / Gas	$
Lodging	$
Tour / Rental	$
Total	$

Describe the activity. Who was there, did you stick to the plan or improvise? How?

Was this a good family bonding activity? How did it get you in the Christmas spirit?

What was the funniest moment at this activity?

What surprised you the most about this activity?

Was there something disappointing? Could the day could have been better? How would you change it?

When you look back at it, what kinds of feelings will you associate with this activity?

What do you want your child(ren) to remember most about this activity?

What is one thing about today you never want to forget?

Rate this activity on a scale of 1-5. Why did you give it this rating?

Activity #27

Where is this activity taking place?

Address:

Activity date:

starts at time:

Need reservations for this activity? Y   N

We made them for
date:
time:
phone:

Lodging:

Address:

Reservations? Y   N

For date

The plan for the activity:

This is what you will be doing. List the details of the activity
_____
_____
_____
_____
_____
_____
_____

What is the hoped for outcome? What do you hope to feel / learn as a family during this activity?
_____
_____
_____

Supplies needed

_____
_____
_____
_____
_____
_____

Budget for this activity:

Food	$
Supplies	$
Entrance Fee	$
Parking / Gas	$
Lodging	$
Tour / Rental	$
Total	$

Describe the activity. Who was there, did you stick to the plan or improvise? How?

Was this a good family bonding activity? How did it get you in the Christmas spirit?

What was the funniest moment at this activity?

What surprised you the most about this activity?

Was there something disappointing? Could the day could have been better? How would you change it?

When you look back at it, what kinds of feelings will you associate with this activity?

What do you want your child(ren) to remember most about this activity?

What is one thing about today you never want to forget?

Rate this activity on a scale of 1-5. Why did you give it this rating?

Activity #28

Where is this activity taking place?

Address:

Activity date:

starts at time:

Need reservations for this activity? Y   N
We made them for
date:
time:
phone:

Lodging:
Address:

Reservations? Y   N
For date

The plan for the activity:

This is what you will be doing. List the details of the activity

_____

_____

_____

_____

_____

_____

_____

What is the hoped for outcome? What do you hope to feel / learn as a family during this activity?

_____

_____

_____

Supplies needed

_____

_____

_____

_____

_____

_____

Budget for this activity:

Food	$
Supplies	$
Entrance Fee	$
Parking / Gas	$
Lodging	$
Tour / Rental	$
Total	$

Describe the activity. Who was there, did you stick to the plan or improvise? How?

Was this a good family bonding activity? How did it get you in the Christmas spirit?

What was the funniest moment at this activity?

What surprised you the most about this activity?

Was there something disappointing? Could the day could have been better? How would you change it?

When you look back at it, what kinds of feelings will you associate with this activity?

What do you want your child(ren) to remember most about this activity?

What is one thing about today you never want to forget?

Rate this activity on a scale of 1-5. Why did you give it this rating?

Activity #29

Where is this activity taking place?

Address:

Activity date:

starts at time:

Need reservations for this activity? Y N
We made them for
date:
time:
phone:

Lodging:
Address:

Reservations? Y N
For date

The plan for the activity:

This is what you will be doing. List the details of the activity
_____
_____
_____
_____
_____
_____
_____
_____

What is the hoped for outcome? What do you hope to feel / learn as a family during this activity?
_____
_____
_____

Supplies needed

_____
_____
_____
_____
_____
_____
_____

Budget for this activity:

Food	$
Supplies	$
Entrance Fee	$
Parking / Gas	$
Lodging	$
Tour / Rental	$
Total	$

Describe the activity. Who was there, did you stick to the plan or improvise? How?

Was this a good family bonding activity? How did it get you in the Christmas spirit?

What was the funniest moment at this activity?

What surprised you the most about this activity?

Was there something disappointing? Could the day could have been better? How would you change it?

When you look back at it, what kinds of feelings will you associate with this activity?

What do you want your child(ren) to remember most about this activity?

What is one thing about today you never want to forget?

Rate this activity on a scale of 1-5. Why did you give it this rating?

Activity #30

Where is this activity taking place?

Address:

Activity date:

starts at time:

Need reservations for this activity? Y N
We made them for
date:
time:
phone:

Lodging:
Address:

Reservations? Y N
For date

The plan for the activity:

This is what you will be doing. List the details of the activity
_____
_____
_____
_____
_____
_____
_____
_____

What is the hoped for outcome? What do you hope to feel / learn as a family during this activity?
_____
_____
_____

Supplies needed

_____
_____
_____
_____
_____
_____

Budget for this activity:

Food	$
Supplies	$
Entrance Fee	$
Parking / Gas	$
Lodging	$
Tour / Rental	$
Total	$

Describe the activity. Who was there, did you stick to the plan or improvise? How?

Was this a good family bonding activity? How did it get you in the Christmas spirit?

What was the funniest moment at this activity?

What surprised you the most about this activity?

Was there something disappointing? Could the day could have been better? How would you change it?

When you look back at it, what kinds of feelings will you associate with this activity?

What do you want your child(ren) to remember most about this activity?

What is one thing about today you never want to forget?

Rate this activity on a scale of 1-5. Why did you give it this rating?

Activity #31

Where is this activity taking place?

Address:

Activity date:

starts at time:

Need reservations for this activity? Y N

We made them for

date:

time:

phone:

Lodging:

Address:

Reservations? Y N

For date

The plan for the activity:

This is what you will be doing. List the details of the activity
_____
_____
_____
_____
_____
_____
_____

What is the hoped for outcome? What do you hope to feel / learn as a family during this activity?
_____
_____
_____

Supplies needed

_____
_____
_____
_____
_____
_____

Budget for this activity:

Food	$
Supplies	$
Entrance Fee	$
Parking / Gas	$
Lodging	$
Tour / Rental	$
Total	$

Describe the activity. Who was there, did you stick to the plan or improvise? How?

_____
_____
_____
_____
_____

Was this a good family bonding activity? How did it get you in the Christmas spirit?

_____
_____

What was the funniest moment at this activity?

_____
_____

What surprised you the most about this activity?

_____
_____

Was there something disappointing? Could the day could have been better? How would you change it?

_____
_____

When you look back at it, what kinds of feelings will you associate with this activity?

_____
_____

What do you want your child(ren) to remember most about this activity?

_____
_____

What is one thing about today you never want to forget?

_____
_____

Rate this activity on a scale of 1-5. Why did you give it this rating?

_____

Activity #32

Where is this activity taking place?

Address:

Activity date:

starts at time:

Need reservations for this activity? Y   N
We made them for
date:
time:
phone:

Lodging:
Address:

Reservations? Y   N
For date

The plan for the activity:

This is what you will be doing. List the details of the activity

_____
_____
_____
_____
_____
_____
_____

What is the hoped for outcome? What do you hope to feel / learn as a family during this activity?

_____
_____
_____

Supplies needed

_____
_____
_____
_____
_____
_____

Budget for this activity:

Food	$
Supplies	$
Entrance Fee	$
Parking / Gas	$
Lodging	$
Tour / Rental	$
Total	$

86

Describe the activity. Who was there, did you stick to the plan or improvise? How?

Was this a good family bonding activity? How did it get you in the Christmas spirit?

What was the funniest moment at this activity?

What surprised you the most about this activity?

Was there something disappointing? Could the day could have been better? How would you change it?

When you look back at it, what kinds of feelings will you associate with this activity?

What do you want your child(ren) to remember most about this activity?

What is one thing about today you never want to forget?

Rate this activity on a scale of 1-5. Why did you give it this rating?

Activity #33

Where is this activity taking place?

Address:

Activity date:

starts at time:

Need reservations for this activity? Y N

We made them for
date:
time:
phone:

Lodging:
Address:

Reservations? Y N
For date

The plan for the activity:

This is what you will be doing. List the details of the activity
_____
_____
_____
_____
_____
_____
_____
_____

What is the hoped for outcome? What do you hope to feel / learn as a family during this activity?
_____
_____
_____

Supplies needed

_____
_____
_____
_____
_____
_____

Budget for this activity:

Food	$
Supplies	$
Entrance Fee	$
Parking / Gas	$
Lodging	$
Tour / Rental	$
Total	$

Describe the activity. Who was there, did you stick to the plan or improvise? How?
_____
_____
_____
_____
_____
_____

Was this a good family bonding activity? How did it get you in the Christmas spirit?
_____
_____

What was the funniest moment at this activity?
_____
_____

What surprised you the most about this activity?
_____
_____

Was there something disappointing? Could the day could have been better? How would you change it?
_____
_____

When you look back at it, what kinds of feelings will you associate with this activity?
_____
_____

What do you want your child(ren) to remember most about this activity?
_____
_____

What is one thing about today you never want to forget?
_____
_____

Rate this activity on a scale of 1-5. Why did you give it this rating?
_____

Activity #34

Where is this activity taking place?

Address:

Activity date:

starts at time:

Need reservations for this activity? Y N
We made them for
date:
time:
phone:

Lodging:

Address:

Reservations? Y N

For date

The plan for the activity:

This is what you will be doing. List the details of the activity

_____
_____
_____
_____
_____
_____
_____

What is the hoped for outcome? What do you hope to feel / learn as a family during this activity?

_____
_____
_____

Supplies needed

_____
_____
_____
_____
_____
_____

Budget for this activity:

Food	$
Supplies	$
Entrance Fee	$
Parking / Gas	$
Lodging	$
Tour / Rental	$
Total	$

Describe the activity. Who was there, did you stick to the plan or improvise? How?

Was this a good family bonding activity? How did it get you in the Christmas spirit?

What was the funniest moment at this activity?

What surprised you the most about this activity?

Was there something disappointing? Could the day could have been better? How would you change it?

When you look back at it, what kinds of feelings will you associate with this activity?

What do you want your child(ren) to remember most about this activity?

What is one thing about today you never want to forget?

Rate this activity on a scale of 1-5. Why did you give it this rating?

Activity #35

Where is this activity taking place?

Address:

Activity date:

starts at time:

Need reservations for this activity? Y   N
We made them for
date:
time:
phone:

Lodging:
Address:

Reservations? Y   N
For date

The plan for the activity:

This is what you will be doing. List the details of the activity
_____
_____
_____
_____
_____
_____
_____
_____

What is the hoped for outcome? What do you hope to feel / learn as a family during this activity?
_____
_____
_____

Supplies needed

_____
_____
_____
_____
_____
_____

Budget for this activity:

Food	$
Supplies	$
Entrance Fee	$
Parking / Gas	$
Lodging	$
Tour / Rental	$
Total	$

Describe the activity. Who was there, did you stick to the plan or improvise? How?

_____
_____
_____
_____
_____
_____

Was this a good family bonding activity? How did it get you in the Christmas spirit?

_____
_____
_____

What was the funniest moment at this activity?

_____
_____
_____

What surprised you the most about this activity?

_____
_____
_____

Was there something disappointing? Could the day could have been better? How would you change it?

_____
_____
_____

When you look back at it, what kinds of feelings will you associate with this activity?

_____
_____
_____

What do you want your child(ren) to remember most about this activity?

_____
_____
_____

What is one thing about today you never want to forget?

_____
_____
_____

Rate this activity on a scale of 1-5. Why did you give it this rating?

_____
_____

Activity #36

Where is this activity taking place?

Address:

Activity date:

starts at time:

Need reservations for this activity? Y N
We made them for
date:
time:
phone:

Lodging:
Address:

Reservations? Y   N
For date

The plan for the activity:

This is what you will be doing. List the details of the activity

_____
_____
_____
_____
_____
_____
_____

What is the hoped for outcome? What do you hope to feel / learn as a family during this activity?

_____
_____
_____

Supplies needed

_____
_____
_____
_____
_____
_____

Budget for this activity:

Food	$
Supplies	$
Entrance Fee	$
Parking / Gas	$
Lodging	$
Tour / Rental	$
Total	$

Describe the activity. Who was there, did you stick to the plan or improvise? How?

_____
_____
_____
_____
_____

Was this a good family bonding activity? How did it get you in the Christmas spirit?

_____
_____

What was the funniest moment at this activity?

_____
_____

What surprised you the most about this activity?

_____
_____

Was there something disappointing? Could the day could have been better? How would you change it?

_____
_____

When you look back at it, what kinds of feelings will you associate with this activity?

_____
_____

What do you want your child(ren) to remember most about this activity?

_____
_____

What is one thing about today you never want to forget?

_____
_____

Rate this activity on a scale of 1-5. Why did you give it this rating?

_____

Activity #37

Where is this activity taking place?

Address:

Activity date:

starts at time:

Need reservations for this activity? Y   N

We made them for
date:
time:
phone:

Lodging:

Address:

Reservations? Y   N

For date

The plan for the activity:

This is what you will be doing. List the details of the activity
_____
_____
_____
_____
_____
_____
_____
_____

What is the hoped for outcome? What do you hope to feel / learn as a family during this activity?
_____
_____
_____

Supplies needed

_____
_____
_____
_____
_____
_____
_____

Budget for this activity:

Food	$
Supplies	$
Entrance Fee	$
Parking / Gas	$
Lodging	$
Tour / Rental	$
Total	$

Describe the activity. Who was there, did you stick to the plan or improvise? How?

_____
_____
_____
_____
_____

Was this a good family bonding activity? How did it get you in the Christmas spirit?

_____
_____
_____

What was the funniest moment at this activity?

_____
_____

What surprised you the most about this activity?

_____
_____
_____

Was there something disappointing? Could the day could have been better? How would you change it?

_____
_____
_____

When you look back at it, what kinds of feelings will you associate with this activity?

_____
_____
_____

What do you want your child(ren) to remember most about this activity?

_____
_____

What is one thing about today you never want to forget?

_____
_____
_____

Rate this activity on a scale of 1-5. Why did you give it this rating?

_____
_____

Activity #38

Where is this activity taking place?

Address:

Activity date:

starts at time:

Need reservations for this activity? Y N
We made them for
date:
time:
phone:

Lodging:
Address:

Reservations? Y N
For date

The plan for the activity:

This is what you will be doing. List the details of the activity

_____
_____
_____
_____
_____
_____
_____

What is the hoped for outcome? What do you hope to feel / learn as a family during this activity?

_____
_____
_____

Supplies needed

_____
_____
_____
_____
_____
_____

Budget for this activity:

Food	$
Supplies	$
Entrance Fee	$
Parking / Gas	$
Lodging	$
Tour / Rental	$
Total	$

Describe the activity. Who was there, did you stick to the plan or improvise? How?

_____
_____
_____
_____
_____

Was this a good family bonding activity? How did it get you in the Christmas spirit?

_____
_____

What was the funniest moment at this activity?

_____
_____

What surprised you the most about this activity?

_____
_____

Was there something disappointing? Could the day could have been better? How would you change it?

_____
_____

When you look back at it, what kinds of feelings will you associate with this activity?

_____
_____

What do you want your child(ren) to remember most about this activity?

_____
_____

What is one thing about today you never want to forget?

_____
_____

Rate this activity on a scale of 1-5. Why did you give it this rating?

Activity #39

Where is this activity taking place?

Address:

Activity date:

starts at time:

Need reservations for this activity? Y N

We made them for
date:
time:
phone:

Lodging:

Address:

Reservations? Y N

For date

The plan for the activity:

This is what you will be doing. List the details of the activity
_____
_____
_____
_____
_____
_____
_____
_____

What is the hoped for outcome? What do you hope to feel / learn as a family during this activity?
_____
_____
_____

Supplies needed

_____
_____
_____
_____
_____
_____
_____

Budget for this activity:

Food	$
Supplies	$
Entrance Fee	$
Parking / Gas	$
Lodging	$
Tour / Rental	$
Total	$

Describe the activity. Who was there, did you stick to the plan or improvise? How?
___
___
___
___
___
___

Was this a good family bonding activity? How did it get you in the Christmas spirit?
___
___
___

What was the funniest moment at this activity?
___
___

What surprised you the most about this activity?
___
___

Was there something disappointing? Could the day could have been better? How would you change it?
___
___
___

When you look back at it, what kinds of feelings will you associate with this activity?
___
___

What do you want your child(ren) to remember most about this activity?
___
___

What is one thing about today you never want to forget?
___
___

Rate this activity on a scale of 1-5. Why did you give it this rating?
___

Activity #40

Where is this activity taking place?

Address:

Activity date:

starts at time:

Need reservations for this activity? Y N
We made them for
date:
time:
phone:

Lodging:
Address:

Reservations? Y   N
For date

The plan for the activity:

This is what you will be doing. List the details of the activity
_____
_____
_____
_____
_____
_____
_____
_____

What is the hoped for outcome? What do you hope to feel / learn as a family during this activity?
_____
_____
_____

Supplies needed

_____
_____
_____
_____
_____
_____

Budget for this activity:

Food	$
Supplies	$
Entrance Fee	$
Parking / Gas	$
Lodging	$
Tour / Rental	$
Total	$

Describe the activity. Who was there, did you stick to the plan or improvise? How?

Was this a good family bonding activity? How did it get you in the Christmas spirit?

What was the funniest moment at this activity?

What surprised you the most about this activity?

Was there something disappointing? Could the day could have been better? How would you change it?

When you look back at it, what kinds of feelings will you associate with this activity?

What do you want your child(ren) to remember most about this activity?

What is one thing about today you never want to forget?

Rate this activity on a scale of 1-5. Why did you give it this rating?

Holiday Movies

We've gathered a list of 40+ holiday movies to cheer your spirits. How many will you watch?

- ❏ It's a Wonderful Life
- ❏ How the Grinch Stole Christmas
- ❏ Polar Express
- ❏ Home Alone 1, 2
- ❏ Elf
- ❏ Jack Frost
- ❏ Scrooged
- ❏ A Christmas Carol (choose your favorite, there are over 24 adaptations!)
- ❏ Miracle on 34th Street
- ❏ Mickey's Once Upon a Christmas
- ❏ The Santa Clause 1, 2, 3
- ❏ I'll Be Home for Christmas (1998)
- ❏ A Christmas Story
- ❏ The Snowman
- ❏ The Muppet Christmas Carol
- ❏ A Charlie Brown Christmas
- ❏ The Nightmare Before Christmas
- ❏ The Shop Around the Corner
- ❏ The Family Man
- ❏ Prancer
- ❏ The Christmas Chronicles, Part 1, 2
- ❏ Jingle All the Way
- ❏ Santa Clause is Coming to Town
- ❏ While You Were Sleeping
- ❏ Mixed Nuts (1994)
- ❏ Christmas in Connecticut
- ❏ Kung Fu Panda Holiday
- ❏ The Bishop's Wife
- ❏ The Little Drummer Boy
- ❏ Trapped in Paradise (1994)
- ❏ Arthur Christmas
- ❏ The Nativity Story
- ❏ A Christmas Tale (2008)
- ❏ Noel (2004)
- ❏ White Christmas
- ❏ Shrek the Halls
- ❏ One Magic Christmas (1985)
- ❏ Frosty the Snowman
- ❏ Deck the Halls
- ❏ The Christmas Spirit
- ❏ A Season for Miracles
- ❏ Jingle Jangle: A Christmas Journey
- ❏ Dolly Parton's Christmas on the Square
- ❏ + anything Hallmark Channel is playing in December
- ❏ + anything Lifetime Channel is playing in December